BIBLE DETECT
LUKE
Puzzle Book

Written by Ros Woodman
Illustrated by Ron Wheeler

Wordsearch Puzzles designed by Chris Woodman
Cover Design by Alister MacInnes
Illustration Ron Wheeler
Printed and bound by Bell and Bain, Glasgow

Published by Christian Focus Publications
Geanies House, Fearn, Tain, Ross-shire, IV20 1TW, Scotland, UK.
www.christianfocus.com email: info@christianfocus.com

Hello, we're Harry and Jess. We're investigating the book of **Luke**, and we've found out a few things about the man who wrote it. We've got Click, our computer mouse, to help. Show us what you found Click.

Luke
A doctor

He travelled with the apostle Paul who planted new churches all over Europe. He wrote this Gospel to a friend called Theophilus. It was carefully researched and written down.

We've found out that Luke met people who'd been with Jesus. He checked that their stories were true ...

Gospel

This is another word for Good News. Some books of the New Testament are called Gospels - Matthew, Mark, Luke and John. It describes the good news that we read in the Bible, which is - Jesus died to save us from our sins.

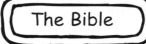

The Bible

This is God's book. He used people to do the actual writing. Prophets, men of God, the disciples - all wrote down or told other people what it was that God said to them. There are two sections. The Old Testament happened before Jesus was born and The New Testament is about Jesus' life, death, resurrection and what his followers did after he went back to heaven. The Old and New Testaments are divided into different sections. The Old Testament is made up of 39 separate books. The New Testament is made up of 27 different books. Each book is divided into smaller sections called chapters. Each chapter is divided into small parts called verses. Books, chapters and verses make it easier to find things in the Bible. When this investigation is finished you will remember that the stories discovered are in the Book of Luke. Luke is the third book of the New Testament. Remember that the Bible is God's word to us. The Gospels are full of true life stories of people that Jesus met. Let's investigate some of them. It's amazing to realise that these things really happened and that every word from God is true!

NEWS OF A BIRTH

Jess and I are investigating about two parents Elizabeth and Zechariah. They were good people and did their best to obey God's commandments. Then one day Zechariah was chosen by lot to enter the sanctuary in the temple. We have discovered that this was a most holy place which only a priest was allowed to enter once a year, and he had to be ceremonially clean before he dared to enter.

That's right, Harry, it was his job to burn incense in God's presence in the sanctuary while a crowd stood outside praying. This time an amazing thing happened- an angel of the Lord appeared! Scary or what? But this is what the angel said: "Don't be afraid, Zechariah! God has heard your prayer. Your wife, Elizabeth will bear you a son!" Now match up the sentences to find out what the angel said about their son. Take each highlighted letter and arrange them to spell the name of their son.

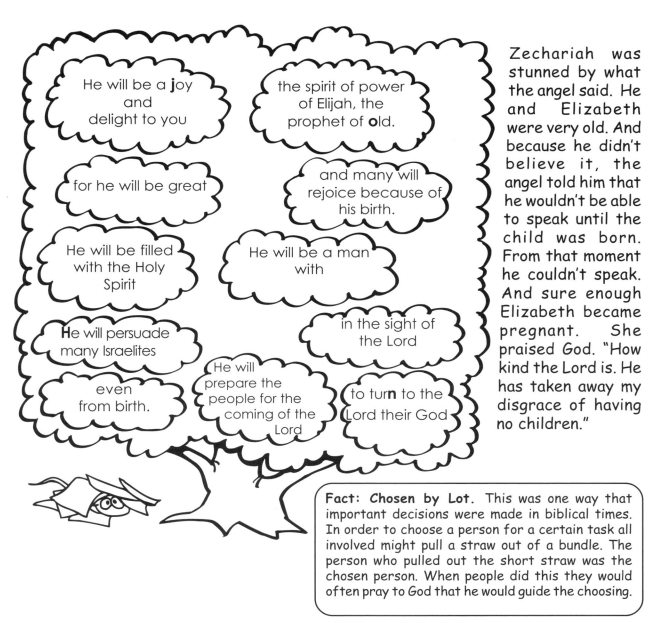

He will be a **j**oy and delight to you

the spirit of power of Elijah, the prophet of **o**ld.

for he will be great

and many will rejoice because of his birth.

He will be filled with the Holy Spirit

He will be a man with

He will persuade many Israelites

in the sight of the Lord

even from birth.

He will prepare the people for the coming of the Lord

to tur**n** to the Lord their God

Zechariah was stunned by what the angel said. He and Elizabeth were very old. And because he didn't believe it, the angel told him that he wouldn't be able to speak until the child was born. From that moment he couldn't speak. And sure enough Elizabeth became pregnant. She praised God. "How kind the Lord is. He has taken away my disgrace of having no children."

Fact: Chosen by Lot. This was one way that important decisions were made in biblical times. In order to choose a person for a certain task all involved might pull a straw out of a bundle. The person who pulled out the short straw was the chosen person. When people did this they would often pray to God that he would guide the choosing.

MARY AND GABRIEL

When Elizabeth was six months pregnant, God sent the angel Gabriel to a village in Galilee. He went to a young woman called Mary and said, "Greetings, favoured woman! The Lord is with you." Mary was confused. She didn't know what he meant.

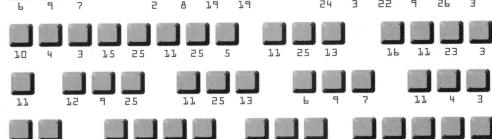

Use the keyboard to work out what he said next. Q=1, W=2 and E=3. Work out the rest before you start the puzzle.

6 9 7   2 8 19 19   24 3 22 9 26 3

10 4 3 15 25 11 25 5   11 25 13   16 11 23 3

11   12 9 25   11 25 13   6 9 7   11 4 3

5 9   25 11 26 3   16 8 26   17 3 12 7 12

Answer: _____

Gabriel told Mary that her son would be great, and would be called the Son of the Most High. Jesus would reign over Israel and his kingdom would never end. It was puzzling for Mary.

She was to have a baby by the Holy Spirit! But she was a woman of faith. Use the keyboard to work out what she said.

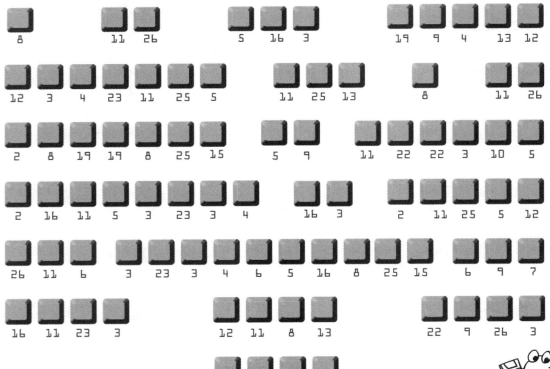

8   11 26   5 16 3   19 9 4 13 12

12 3 4 23 11 25 5   11 25 13   8   11 26

2 8 19 19 8 25 15   5 9   11 22 22 3 10 5

2 16 11 5 3 23 3 4   16 3   2 11 25 5 12

26 11 6 3 23 3 4 6 5 16 8 25 15   6 9 7

16 11 23 3   12 11 8 13   22 9 26 3

5 4 7 3

Answer: _____

4

MARY VISITS ELIZABETH AND ZECHARIAH

LUKE 1: 39-45

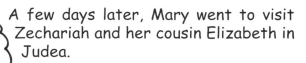

A few days later, Mary went to visit Zechariah and her cousin Elizabeth in Judea.

Can you help Mary find her way to Elizabeth and Zechariah's house.

When Mary arrived an amazing thing happened. As she greeted her cousin, Elizabeth's baby leaped for joy from within her and she was filled with the Holy Spirit. "You are blessed by God above all women," said Elizabeth, "and your child is blessed. What an honour this is that the mother of my Lord should visit me."

THE BIRTH OF JESUS

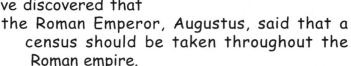

Jess and I have been finding out more about what went on before Jesus' birth. And we've discovered that the Roman Emperor, Augustus, said that a census should be taken throughout the Roman empire.

Luke 2:1-7

Everyone had to go to their own towns to register for the census, and Joseph and Mary travelled to Bethlehem. While they were there, Mary gave birth to Jesus and she wrapped him in strips of cloth and laid him in a manger.

SHEPHERDS AND ANGELS

What differences can you spot between the three cards?

Luke 2: 8-20

That night in the fields outside Bethlehem, some shepherds were guarding their flocks of sheep.

Suddenly an angel appeared. "Don't be afraid," he said. "I bring you good news of great joy for everyone. The Saviour who is the Messiah, the Lord, has been born tonight in Bethlehem."

The angel told them that they would find the baby lying in a manger wrapped in strips of cloth. Then suddenly, the angel was joined by a host of others, praising God.

"Glory to God in the Highest Heaven and peace on earth."

JESUS IS PRESENTED AT THE TEMPLE

Luke 2:21-40

After Jesus was born, Mary and Joseph took him to the temple in Jerusalem to be dedicated to the Lord. And while they were there, Mary and Joseph met two very Godly people. Let's take a look at their files to find out more...

Anna - *Family:* **Daughter of Phanuel of the tribe of Asher.** *Marital Status:* **Widow** *Age:* **84** *Personal details:* **Never leaves the temple. Stays there day and night worshipping God with fasting and prayer.**

Simeon - *Personal Details:* **A man filled with the Holy Spirit. Eagerly expects the Messiah to come. The Holy Spirit has told him he will not die until he has seen the Lord's Messiah.**

As soon as they saw Jesus, they knew who he was. Anna began praising God and talking to everyone about Jesus. Simeon took Jesus in his arms and began to speak about who Jesus was and what he would do. Fill in the gaps to find out what Simeon said. Then re-arrange missing letters to spell out a name given to describe Jesus.

Answer: _____

Lord, now I can d_part in peace! For _y eyes _ave _een your salvation which you have prepared in the light of all people, a light to reve_l God to the nat_ons, and he is the glory of your people I_rael.

Then Simeon blessed Jesus. Find out what he said. Take the letters from the word IMMANUEL (meaning God with us) and use them to fill in the gaps.

This child is destined to cause the falling and rising of _any in _srael, _nd to be a sign that wil_ be spoken agai_st, so that the thoughts of _any h_arts will be revealed. And a sword will pierce your own so_l too.

7

JESUS SPEAKS WITH THE TEACHERS

While he was still young, Jesus surprised people with the things he did. Even his Mum and Dad! I mean, look at the time when he went to Jerusalem with them to celebrate a festival. He was twelve years old... Nothing out of the ordinary at first. But after the celebrations the people set out for the return journey to Nazareth. That is, everyone except for Jesus. Well, Mary and Joseph didn't miss him at first. They thought he was with friends or relatives among the other travellers. Until he didn't turn up that evening! And then the search was on. In the end they had to go back to Jerusalem, where they found him three days later – in the temple. He was sitting among the religious leaders discussing deep questions with them. And all the people who heard him were amazed at his understanding and answers. Mary and Joseph didn't know what to think. "Son, why have you done this to us? We've been frantic, searching for you all over the place," they said. But Jesus said, "But why did you need to search? You should have known I would be in my Father's house." Then they returned to Nazareth, where Jesus grew in wisdom. And everyone, including God, loved him.

Answer the following questions. The column going down will show the name of the festival they were celebrating.
1. What sort of questions?
2. Mary and Joseph felt this way when they couldn't find Jesus.
3. The people went to Jerusalem to celebrate one.
4. The people who heard Jesus were amazed by them.
5. Another name for the place of worship - _ _ _ _ _ of God
6. Jesus' parents thought he was with them.
7. Where they found Jesus.
8. Jesus' home town.

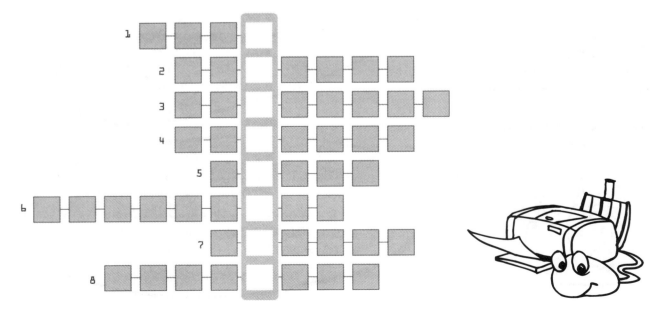

8

JOHN THE BAPTIST PREPARES THE WAY

Luke 3: 1-22

So now back to Jesus' cousin, John. Remember? Well, everything that the angel had told Elizabeth came true - John the Baptist was used by God to tell everyone that the Messiah was coming soon. "Someone is coming who is much greater than I am," he said, "and I am not even worthy to be his slave."

And John's words also came true. One day, when he was baptising crowds of people, Jesus came and was baptised too. The Holy Spirit came down on him like a dove and a voice spoke from heaven.

Can you work out what the voice said? Insert every second letter in the spaces to work it out.

IOTNHAYNODUI YAOMUFAURLELMYYPBLEELAOSVEEDDWS

___ ___ __ _____ ___ ___ _ __ _____ _____ ____ ___

Then Jesus went into the desert where the devil tempted him for forty days. He didn't eat anything and was really hungry.

But Satan still didn't get the better of him. He went away, deciding to wait for another chance to try and get at Jesus. Let's keep going to find out what happened next...

JESUS REJECTED AT NAZARETH

Luke 4:1-30

Jesus Christ was filled with the power of the Holy Spirit and he went back to Galilee. And soon he became well known. He taught in the synagogues and everyone praised him.

Nazareth was Jesus' boyhood home, and one Sabbath day he went to the synagogue there. When he stood up to read the Scriptures, the scroll containing the messages of Isaiah the prophet was handed to him. Jesus unrolled the scroll to the place where it says this:

(Fill in the gaps by using the code pictures.)
The Spirit of the Lord is upon me,
For he has appointed me
to preach _ _ _ _   _ _ _ _
to the poor.
He has sent me to proclaim
that captives will be released,
that the blind will see,
that the deaf will hear,
that the _ _ _ _ _ _ _ _ _ _
will be freed
from their oppressors
and that the time of the Lord's
favour has come.

Jesus rolled up the scroll, handed it back to the attendant and sat down. He said, "This scripture has come true today before your eyes!"

Everyone who was there spoke well of Jesus. They were amazed by the things he said, saying, "How is this possible? Isn't he Joseph's son?"

Then Jesus said, "you will probably tell me the proverb, 'Doctor heal yourself,' and what you mean by this is, 'Why don't you do miracles here like you did in Capernaum?' But the truth is, no-one is accepted in his own home town." Then Jesus talked about the prophet Elijah and how when there was no rain for three and a half years, he was sent to help a widow who was a foreigner. He also talked about Elisha, who healed Naaman, a Syrian. Naaman was also a foreigner, a non Jew.

When they heard this, the crowd of people in the synagogue were furious. They jumped up and dragged Jesus with them to the edge of a hill on which the city was built. They intended to push him over the cliff, but he slipped away through the crowd and left them.

Across

1. Jesus unrolled it.
5. Jesus was appointed to do this.
7. Jesus read the writings of this prophet.
9. The Lord's _ _ _ _ _ _ has come.
12. Something good which was preached.
13. They mobbed Jesus.
14. Opposite of "she".
15. When had Scripture come true?
19. The downtrodden would be this.
20. Naaman's healer.

Down

1. Jesus had this power.
The power of the Holy _ _ _ _ _ _
2. Jesus did this from the scroll.
3. It didn't come for over 3 years.
4. A name for Jesus.
6. Went back.
8. People felt this when they heard Jesus.
10. A type of news.
11. Jesus slipped _ _ _ _.
13. Jesus was nearly pushed over it.
14. A prophet is not accepted in this town.
16. Sharp or sour
17. To cure/make healthy.
18. The blind will do this.

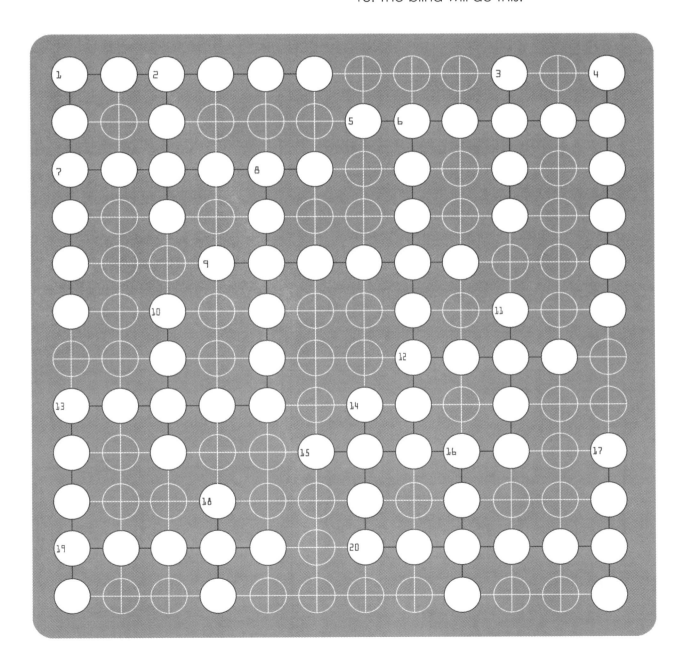

11

JESUS CASTS OUT A DEMON

We've learned that Jesus spoke with such authority that people kept on being amazed.

That's right. I mean, take the time when he went to the synagogue in Capernaum one day. A man was there and he was possessed by a demon. And he began shouting at Jesus.

"Go away! Why are you bothering us, Jesus of Nazareth? Have you come to destroy us? I know who you are – the Holy One sent from God."

Jesus just said, "Be silent! Come out of the man." And as the crowd watched, the demon threw the man to the floor and left without hurting him further.

Well, the people were stunned. Put the jigsaw pieces together to find out what they said.

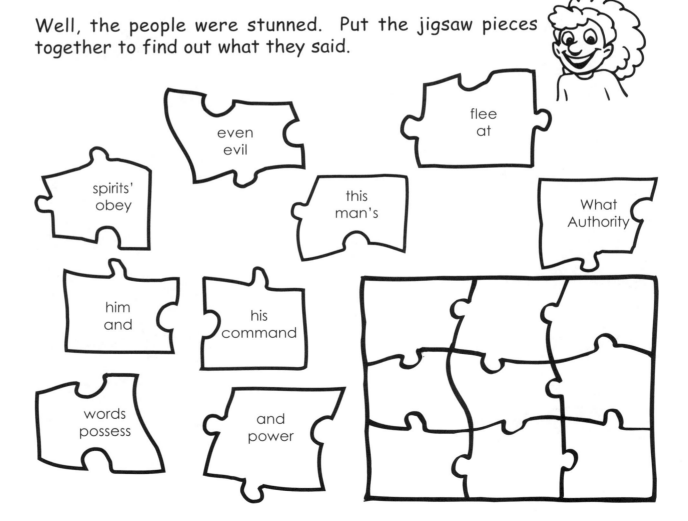

THE FIRST DISCIPLES

Luke 5:1-11

Here's a great story. Read the print-out to find out more about the first disciples.

Jesus was down by the shore of the Sea of Galilee one day. Lots of people were pressing in on him as he preached, and it began to get pretty uncomfortable. Just by the water's edge were two empty fishing boats. The owners were close by, mending their nets, so Jesus climbed into one and asked them to push it out into the water, then he carried on preaching. When Jesus had finished speaking, he said to Simon, one of the fishermen, "Go out where it's deeper and let down your nets, and you'll catch lots of fish." Simon was not sure about this. "Master," he said, "we worked hard all last night and didn't catch a thing. But, if you say so we'll try again." It wasn't long before the nets were so full of fish they began to tear. The fishermen shouted to their partners in the other boat, and soon both were filled with fish and nearly sinking.

Simon Peter fell to his knees in front of Jesus, "Oh Lord, please leave me. I'm too much of a sinner to be around you." He and his partners James and John were awe-struck by the size of the catch.

Match the fish shapes and fill in the blanks to find out what Jesus said in reply.

Answer: _____

13

JESUS CALLS LEVI

Wow! That was quite something! And there's more, as you'll see below.

One day, Jesus saw a man called Levi sitting at his tax collection booth. "Come, be my disciple," he said. So Levi got up, left everything and followed Jesus. Levi invited Jesus to a banquet at his home and many of his fellow tax collectors and friends were there too. But the Pharisees and their teachers of religious law complained to the disciples and said, "Why do you eat and drink with such scum?"

Find out what Jesus said by using the words in the grapes to fill in the gaps.

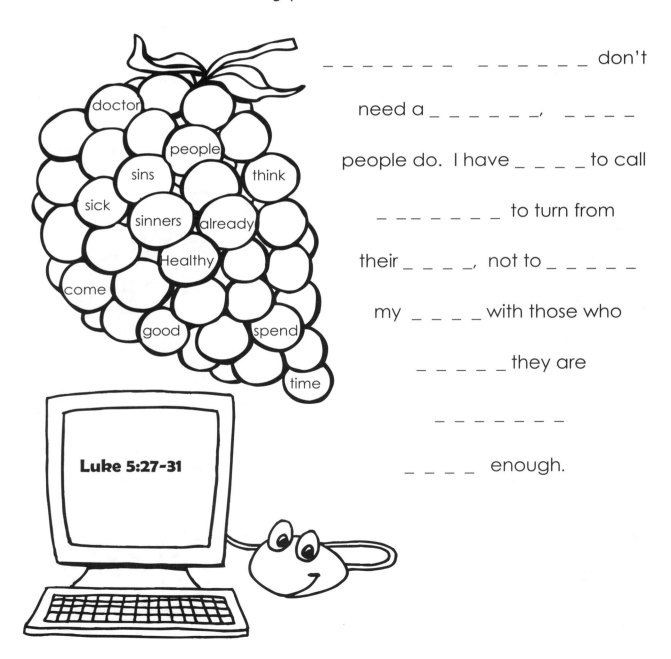

_ _ _ _ _ _ _ _ _ _ _ _ _ don't

need a _ _ _ _ _ _ _, _ _ _ _

people do. I have _ _ _ _ to call

_ _ _ _ _ _ _ to turn from

their _ _ _ _, not to _ _ _ _ _

my _ _ _ _ with those who

_ _ _ _ _ _ they are

_ _ _ _ _ _ _

_ _ _ _ enough.

Luke 5:27-31

Words in grapes: doctor, people, sins, think, sick, sinners, already, Healthy, come, good, spend, time

14

JESUS CHOOSES TWELVE APOSTLES

One day, Jesus went to a mountain to pray. He prayed to God through the night, and early the next morning he called together all the disciples and chose twelve to be apostles. Click has downloaded a puzzle for us - use the code to work out the names of the apostles.

a e i o u b c d h j l m n p r s t w r

A E I O U   B C D H J L M N P R S T W R

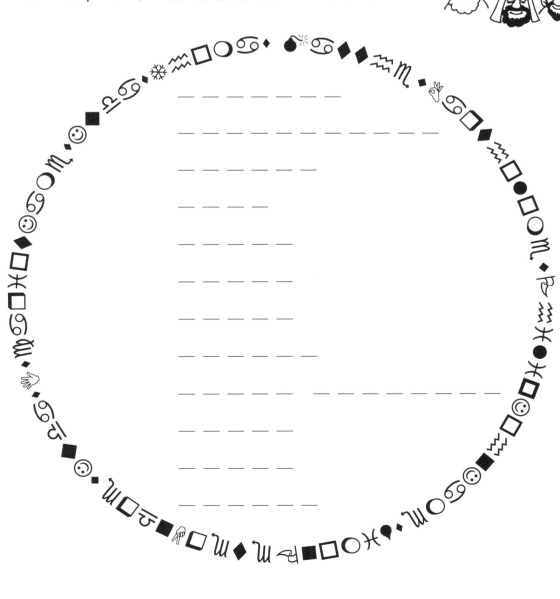

CROWDS FOLLOW JESUS

Luke 6: 7-19

Jesus and the disciples came down the slopes of the mountain to a place where crowds of people were waiting for them. They had come from many different places to hear Jesus. Look at the map to see some of the places that are mentioned in chapter 6 of Luke's gospel. - But you will have to replace the vowels.

They had come to hear Jesus and to be healed, and while they were there Jesus also cast out many evil spirits.

Everyone was trying to touch Jesus because healing power went out from him, and they were all healed.

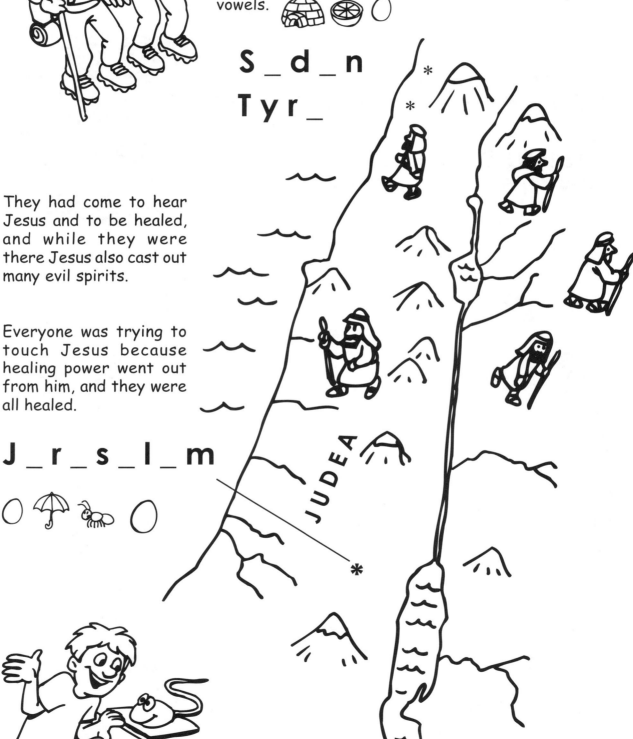

S _ d _ n

T y r _

J _ r _ s _ l _ m

JUDEA

16

THE FAITH OF A ROMAN OFFICER

It wasn't just the Jews who were affected by Jesus as this next story shows.

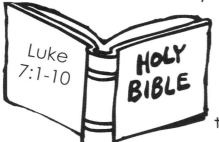

Jesus spent some time preaching, and then he went back to Capernaum. While he was there, some Jewish leaders came to him and asked for Jesus' help.

Luke 7:1-10

HOLY BIBLE

A highly valued slave of a Roman officer was sick and near to death. The leaders begged Jesus to come and heal him. "If anyone deserves help it's this officer," they said. "He loves the Jews and even built a synagogue for us."

Jesus went with them, but before they arrived at the house, the officer sent some friends to Jesus with a message. "Lord, don't trouble yourself by coming to my home because I am not worthy of such an honour. I am not even worthy to come and meet you. Just say the word from where you are and my servant will be healed. I know this because I am under the authority of my superior officers. And I have authority over my soldiers. I say 'Go' and they go, or 'Come' and they come. If I say to my slaves 'Do this' or 'Do that' they do it." Jesus was amazed when he heard this, and turning to the crowd he said, "I tell you ..."

Use the clocks to work out what Jesus said.

8am 7am, 12am, 9pm, 4am 1pm, 2pm, 7pm 5am, 2pm, 8pm, 1pm, 3am

6pm, 8pm, 2am, 7am 6am, 5pm, 4am, 12am, 7pm 5am, 12am, 8am, 7pm, 7am

4am, 9pm, 4am, 1pm 8am, 1pm 8am, 6pm, 5pm, 12am, 4am, 11am

Answer: _____

When the officer's friends went back to the house they found the slave completely healed.

JESUS RAISES A WIDOW'S SON

Jesus was well known all over Judaea and past its borders. The more we read, the more we find out how great he was. This story happened just outside a village called Nain. In those days widows faced real hardship. They were often very poor and relied on others to survive. This woman had lost her only son, and now she had no-one to care for her in her old age.

Luke 7:11-17

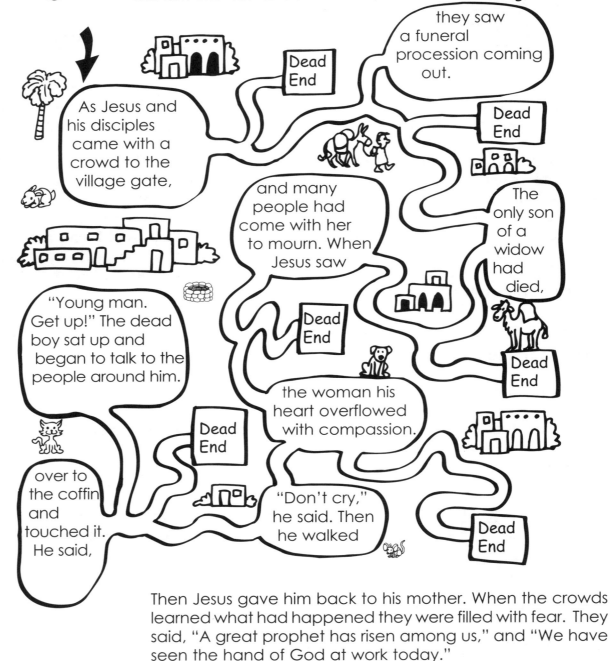

Then Jesus gave him back to his mother. When the crowds learned what had happened they were filled with fear. They said, "A great prophet has risen among us," and "We have seen the hand of God at work today."

Can you find the following hidden on the page: a cat (something the cat might chase) a dog (and something a dog might chase), a donkey (and somewhere it would get some shade) a camel (and a place it would get some water from).

JESUS ANOINTED BY A SINFUL WOMAN

A Pharisee asked Jesus to come to his home for a meal one day. So Jesus accepted his invitation, and sat down to eat. While Jesus was there, an immoral woman came to him, bringing a beautiful jar filled with expensive perfume. Everyone saw her kneeling beside Jesus. She was weeping, and as her tears fell onto his feet, she wiped them off with her hair. Then she kept kissing his feet and putting perfume on them. Jesus' host saw what was happening, and he said to himself, "This proves that Jesus isn't a prophet. If God had really sent him, he would know that this woman is a sinner."

Luke 7:36-50

Then Jesus spoke, answering his thoughts. "Simon," he said, "I have something to say to you." "All right, Teacher. Go ahead," said Simon. Then Jesus told a story.

"A man loaned some money to two people. He gave 500 pieces of silver to one and 50 pieces to the other as a loan. However, neither of them could repay him, so he forgave them both and cancelled their debts. Who do you think loved him more after that?"

Simon replied, "I suppose the one who had the larger debt cancelled."

"That's right," Jesus said. Then he turned to the woman and said to Simon, "You see this woman kneeling here. When I entered your home you didn't offer me water to wash the dust from my feet. She has washed them with her tears and wiped them with her hair. You didn't give me a kiss of greeting, but from the moment I came in she hasn't stopped kissing my feet. You didn't show me the courtesy of anointing my head with olive oil, but she has anointed my feet with rare perfume. I tell you, her sins are many, but they have been forgiven, so she has shown me much love. But a person who is forgiven little shows only little love." Then Jesus said to the woman,

Replace the missing letters with the vowels - the different faces will give you a clue to what letter should go where.

Y__ __ r s __ ns __ r __ f__ rg __ v __ n.

The men at the table said among themselves, "Who does this man think he is, going around forgiving sins?" And Jesus said to the woman, "Your faith has saved you. Go in peace."

CROSSWORD

Across

1. Clear liquid.
3. Another word meaning on your knees.
5. Jesus was invited to one.
6. To cleanse.
8. The place where a person lives.
9. "If God had really _ _ _ _ him."
11. The woman's faith did this for her.
13. Jesus did this before eating.
15. It was cancelled.
16. A fruit used to make oil.
18. To chew and swallow.
20. Silver was given as one.
24. Opposite of above.
25. The perfume container.
26. It saved the woman .
27. A small question word. _ _ (see 9 across)
28. Went into.
32. She wiped her tears with it.
33. Used to unlock something.
34. Jesus came to do this for sinners.

Down

1. A female
2. They fell onto Jesus' feet.
3. Jesus was not given one.
4. A kiss was given as one.
6. Opposite of laughing.
7. Oil to anoint what?
10. The men sat here.
12. Perfume was used for this purpose.
14. The woman was this.
17. The Pharisee gave this instruction to Jesus (2,5).
19. Jesus and the people did this around the table.
21. The woman showed much of this.
22. "You didn't _ _ _ _ _ me water."
23. The name of the Pharisee.
24. He forgave them _ _ _ _.
29. The perfume was this.
30. Something to be washed off the feet.
31. To speak.
32. Opposite of She.

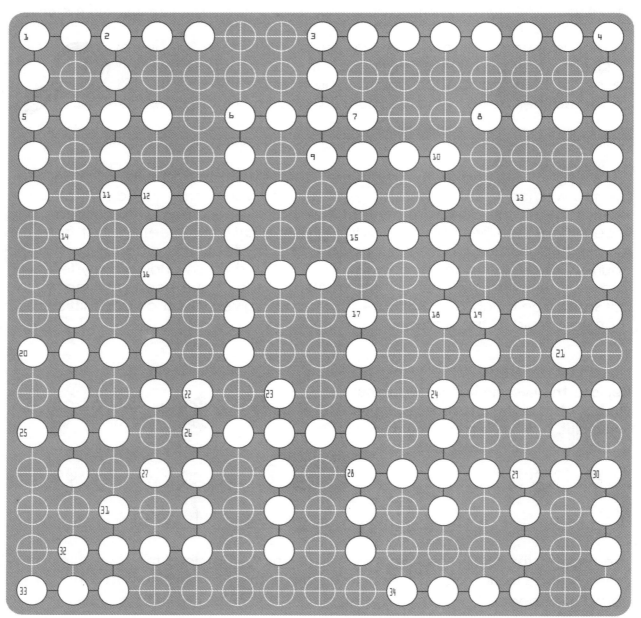

WOMEN WHO FOLLOWED JESUS

We've been finding out more about what happened next.

Yes, and we've discovered that Jesus and his disciples went on a tour of nearby cities and villages.

Follow the lines to find out Jesus' aim.

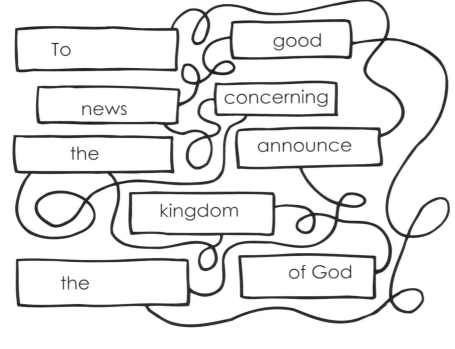

To good

news concerning

the announce

kingdom

the of God

Some women came with Jesus. Write down the first letter of each object in the picture and spell their names.

_ _ _ _ _ _ _ _ _ _ _ _ _ _ _ _ _

_ _ _ _ _ _ _

Luke 8: 1-3

_ _ _ _ _ _ _ _ _ _ _ _

_ _ _ _ _ _ _ _ _ _

JESUS HEALS IN RESPONSE TO FAITH

Luke 8: 40-56

In Jesus' time, women and girls weren't thought to be important. But Jesus showed that men, women, boys and girls are all loved by God. Click has faxed a story about a woman and a twelve year old girl whose lives were changed by Jesus. It began when a leader of the local synagogue begged Jesus for help as his only daughter was dying. Here's what happened...

As Jesus walked, people pressed in on him from all sides. A woman was in the crowd who had been bleeding for twelve years. She had spent all that she had on doctors. No one could cure her, but her hope was rising again. Desperately, she pushed her way through the people, searching for Jesus. And there he was! If she could just get a little closer and touch his robe.

"Who touched me?" asked Jesus. "But Master," a disciple said. "This whole crowd is pressing in on you!" "Someone deliberately touched me. I felt healing power go out from me." Immediately the woman knew she had been healed and could feel the excitement welling up inside her. But Jesus had noticed. Perhaps if she kept quiet he would move on. The woman began to tremble. She was afraid. Jesus knew! So the woman owned up and told Jesus everything. But Jesus wasn't angry. His face showed care and concern. He was pleased. "Daughter," he said, "Your faith has made you well. Go in Peace."

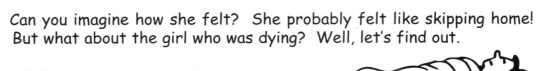

Can you imagine how she felt? She probably felt like skipping home! But what about the girl who was dying? Well, let's find out.

While Jesus was speaking a messenger arrived to say that the young girl had died. "There is no point in troubling the teacher now," the messenger said. The worst had happened. They were too late! "Don't be afraid..." Jesus said. "Just trust me and she will be all right." They could hear the sounds of weeping and wailing as they reached the house, but Jesus spoke again. "Stop the weeping. She isn't dead. She's only asleep." The mother and father followed Jesus and three of the disciples, Peter, James and John, into the room where the girl lay. Jesus looked at her, stretched out his hand and said, "Get up little girl," Straight away life returned to her and she was standing up! It was amazing! "Give her something to eat," said Jesus as they watched, overwhelmed by what he had done. And he insisted that they told no one what had happened.

Can you answer the following questions? The vertical column will then reveal the name of the girl's father.

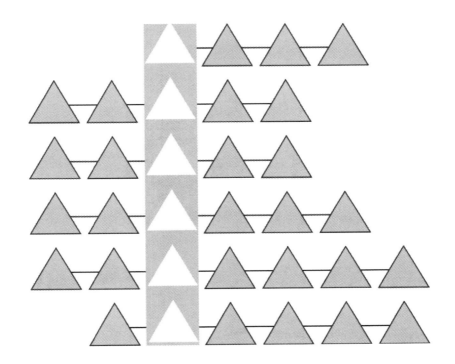

1. A disciple who came into the room with Jesus.

2. "Go in _ _ _ _ _.

3. It had made the woman well.

4. The woman felt this when she realised that Jesus knew.

5. The woman did this to Jesus' robe.

6. The girl wasn't dead, but _ _ _ _ _ _.

JESUS SENDS OUT THE TWELVE DISCIPLES

We've been finding out that Jesus wanted to teach his disciples to do the things that he did.

Click has found another puzzle for the Bible Detectives to do.

Come on everybody, take a look!

Luke 9: 1-6

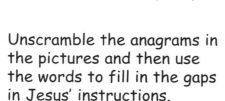

Unscramble the anagrams in the pictures and then use the words to fill in the gaps in Jesus' instructions.

t o c a

lakwngi cksti

sagemse

Traveller's

gab

e f t e

ustd

nomye

ehom

odof

Don't take a _ _ _ _ _ _ _ _ _ _ _ _ _ or a traveller's _ _ _, nor _ _ _ _, nor _ _ _ _ _. Not even an extra _ _ _ _. When you enter the village, be a guest in only one_ _ _ _. If the people of the village won't receive your _ _ _ _ _ _ _ when you enter it, shake off its _ _ _ _ from your _ _ _ _ as you leave. It's a sign that you have abandoned that village to its fate.

SAYINGS OF JESUS

It took a while before the disciples realised who Jesus was. When Jesus asked them who people said he was, Peter declared that he was the Christ. God had promised the Jews long ago that a saviour would come to them, and now here he was among them. This is what Jesus said about himself.

"The Son of Man must suffer many things and be rejected by the elders, chief priests and teachers of the law, and he must be killed, and on the third day be raised to life."

Jesus warned the disciples not to tell anyone. Then he spoke to them all. Find out what he said by putting the following words into the right order.

Luke 9: 21-24

HOLY BIBLE

If any

be my

wants to

of you

followers

put aside

you must

selfish ambition

and follow me

life

keep

lose

find

give

true

If you try to _ _ _ _ your _ _ _ _ for yourself, you will _ _ _ _ it. But if you _ _ _ _ up your life for me, you will _ _ _ _ _ _ _ _ life.

Fill in the gaps using the words from around the edge of the life belt.

THE TRANSFIGURATION

Hey! Check this out. It's awesome.

Jesus took Peter, James and John to a mountain to pray. While he was praying his face changed and his clothes became dazzling white. Then Moses and Elijah appeared and began talking with Jesus. They spoke about how Jesus would fulfil God's plan by dying in Jerusalem.

Luke 9: 28-36

The three disciples were very tired and had fallen asleep. When they woke up they saw Jesus' glory and the two men standing with him. And as Moses and Elijah were starting to leave, Peter, who didn't know what he was saying blurted out, "Master, this is wonderful! We will make three shelters – one for each of you. As he was saying this, a cloud came over them and terror gripped them as it covered them. Then a voice in the cloud said:

Take each letter with a star and put them together to find out what the voice said.

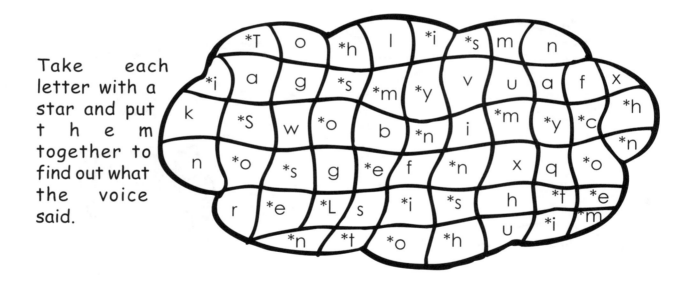

Answer: _____

When the voice died away, Jesus stood there alone. And the disciples didn't tell anyone what they had seen until long after it had happened.

Find the following hidden in the cloud: Peter, James, John, Jesus, Moses, Elijah

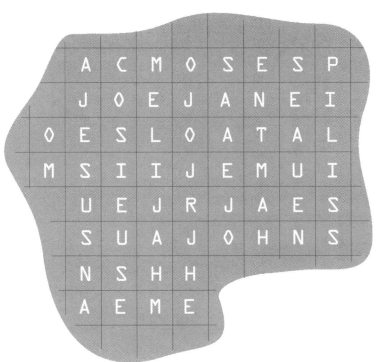

```
A C M O S E S P
J O E J A N E I
O E S L O A T A L
M S I I J E M U I
U E J R J A E S
S U A J O H N S
N S H H
A E M E
```

THE COST OF FOLLOWING JESUS

Luke 9:57-62

HOLY BIBLE

Some time later, as Jesus and his followers were walking along, a man said, "I will follow you no matter where you go." Can you work out what he replied?

A = E = I = O = U =

F O X E S   H A V E   D E N S   T O

L O V E   I N   A N D   B I R D S

H A V E   N E S T S   B U T   E

T H E   S O N   O F   M A N   H A V E

N O   H O M E   O F   M Y   O W N

Jesus wasn't saying this to make the person feel sorry for him. He just wanted him to understand that life won't always be easy for the person who chooses to follow him.

Then Jesus said to another person, "Come, be my disciple." The man agreed, but he said, "Lord, first let me go home and bury my father." Jesus replied:

LET THIS WHO ARE

SPIRITUALLY DEAD

CARE FOR THEIR OWN

DEAD

This doesn't mean that his father was already dead. Jesus wanted people to realise that following him is not something to be put off till later.

Then another said, "Yes Lord, I will follow you, but first let me say good-bye to my family." But Jesus said:

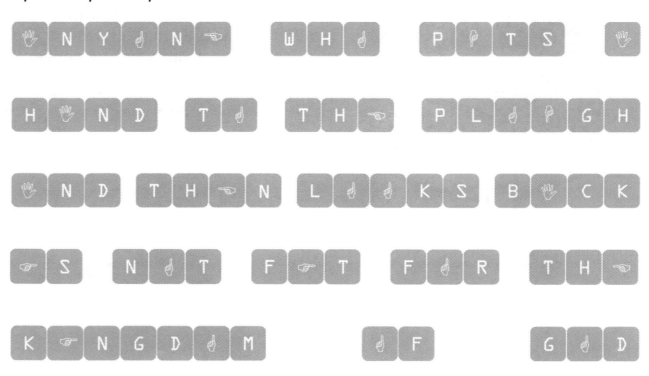

ANYONE WHO PUTS

HAND TO THE PLOUGH

AND THEN LOOKS BACK

IS NOT FIT FOR THE

KINGDOM OF GOD

Jesus won't accept half-hearted followers. When someone ploughs a field, he must concentrate fully or the furrow will be crooked. If we belong to Jesus, we mustn't let other things distract us from following him.

28

THE GOOD SAMARITAN

Luke 10: 25-37

It seems that wherever he went, People tried to test Jesus.

And one day an expert in religious law had a go. He asked Jesus what he must do to receive eternal life. Jesus said, "What does the law of Moses say?"

Fit the jigsaw pieces together and find out what he replied.

God with all

And love your neighbour

and all your mind

all your strength

your heart,

all your soul,

the Lord your

You must love

as yourself.

Answer: _____

"Right," said Jesus. "So do this and you will live.

"But who is my neighbour?" the man asked. So Jesus told this story

Can you spot the differences?

Can you spot the difference in each pair of pictures

A Jewish man was travelling from Jerusalem to Jericho, and he was attacked by bandits. They stripped him of his clothes and money, then left him half dead beside the road.

A Jewish priest came along, but when he saw the man lying there he crossed the road and passed him by.

A temple assistant walked over and saw him lying there, but he, too, crossed to the other side.

Then a Samaritan came along. He was despised by the Jews. When he saw the man he was moved with pity. He knelt beside the man, soothed his wounds with medicine and bandaged them.

He put the man on his donkey and took him to an inn where he took care of him. The next day he gave the innkeeper two pieces of silver to take care of the man. "If his bill is higher than that," he said, "I will pay the difference next time I am here."

JESUS CRITICISES THE RELIGIOUS LEADERS

Click has found a new story about Jesus. Take a look.

Luke 11:37-53

One day when Jesus was speaking, a Pharisee invited him home for a meal. So Jesus went in and took his place at the table. When he sat down to eat, Jesus didn't perform the ceremonial washing required by custom, and it amazed his host. Jesus said to him, "You Pharisees are careful to clean the outside of the cup and the dish, but on the inside you are still filthy. You are full of greed and wickedness. You fools! Didn't God make the inside as well as the outside? So give the things you greedily possess to the needy and you will be clean all over." Jesus went on, "How terrible it will be for you Pharisees. You carefully tithe even the smallest part of your income. But you completely forget about justice and the love of God. Yes, you should tithe, but you should do the important things too. How terrible it will be for you Pharisees. You love the seats of honour in the synagogues and the respectful greetings from everyone as you walk through the markets. You are like hidden graves in the field. People walk on them, but they don't know the corruption they are stepping on."

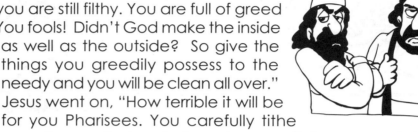

"You have insulted us, Teacher," said an expert in religious law, and Jesus replied sounding stern, "Yes, how terrible it will be for you experts in religious law. You crush people beneath impossible religious demands and you don't even try to help lift their burden. You build tombs for the prophets your ancestors killed long ago. And you agree with your ancestors, for you would have done the same thing yourselves. God in his wisdom said about you, 'I will send prophets and apostles to them and they will kill some and persecute others.'" Jesus went on, "Your generation will be held responsible for the murder of all God's prophets from the creation of the world – from the murder of Abel to the murder of Zechariah, who was killed between the altar and the sanctuary. It's you experts in religious law who hide the key to knowledge from the people. You don't enter the kingdom and you prevent others from entering." By the time Jesus had finished speaking, the Pharisees and teachers of religious law were furious. And from then on, they grilled him with hostile questions and tried to trap him into saying something they could use against him. **Now we have a crossword to do - so come on Detectives let's get on with this investigation! Most of the clues can be found in the story - but some you will have to work out on your own. The non story clues are all in bold.**

Fact Box: Tithe - To give 10% or a tenth of all that you earn to God.

Across

1. Jesus' enemies tried to do this to him.
3. A crime against God's prophets.
6. The opposite of death.
8. Jesus took his place at it.
11. A grape bearing plant.
12. Everyone/everything.
14. He was murdered.
15. A piece of material worn usually by men around the neck.
16. A name/title given to Jesus.
18. Jesus' heavenly father.
19. A - - - to knowledge hidden by experts.
20. It was cleaned on the outside.
23. People who were skilled in religious law.
24. To keep from being seen.
28. Cleaned on the outside.
31. "You - - - - the seats of honour".
32. Jesus did this at the table.
33. Zechariah was killed near it.
34. A compass direction.
35. The Pharisees walked through them.
36. Jesus' attitude towards the Pharisees.

Down

1. The Pharisees did this with their income.
2. Opposite of receive.
3. Adult males.
4. Opposite of life.
5. Someone who governs.
7. The Pharisees were this on the inside.
9. "You - - - - - tombs for the prophets.
10. Jesus sat down to do this.
13. Not to tell the truth.
17. "You - - - - - people beneath impossible religious demands".
18. Jesus accused the Pharisees of this.
21. - - - - - - - - of the world.
22. To weep.
25. Where were they filthy?
26. The centre of an apple.
27. Places of honour.
29. A thought which may include a plan.
30. A bird of prey.
31. Rules made by those in authority.

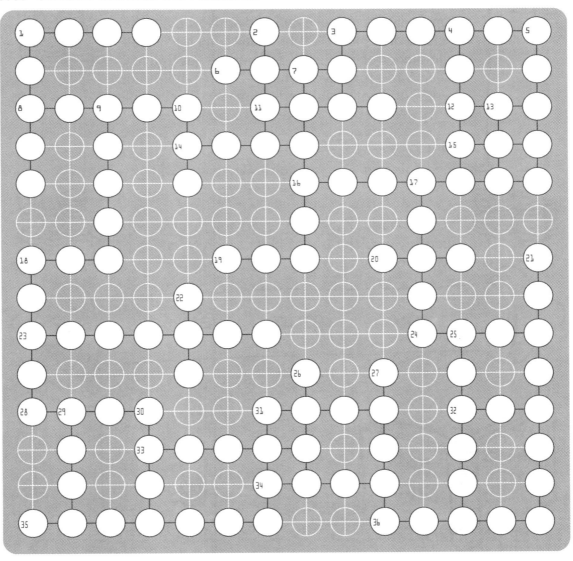

THE RICH FOOL

The more we find out about Jesus, the more we realise how wise he was.

Yeah. And people liked to come to him with their problems, just like the man in the next story. To fill in the gaps look at the letters beneath the story. Go one letter back in the alphabet and you will work out the correct words

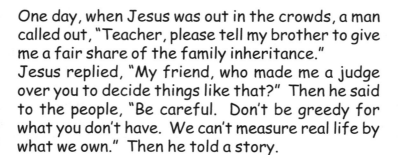

One day, when Jesus was out in the crowds, a man called out, "Teacher, please tell my brother to give me a fair share of the family inheritance."
Jesus replied, "My friend, who made me a judge over you to decide things like that?" Then he said to the people, "Be careful. Don't be greedy for what you don't have. We can't measure real life by what we own." Then he told a story.

A rich man had a farm which produced very fine crops. His barns were full to overflowing, so he decided on a plan. "I'll tear down my barns and build bigger ones," he said, "then I'll have plenty of room to store everything. I'll sit back, take it easy, and eat, drink and be merry. There will be plenty stored away for years to come."

But God said to the man, "_ _ _   _ _ _ _! You are going to _ _ _ tonight. Then who will get it all?"

Jesus said, "A person is a fool to store up earthly wealth but not have a rich friendship with God."

zpv   gppm   ejf

Luke 12: 13-21   HOLY BIBLE

34

JESUS HEALS ON THE SABBATH

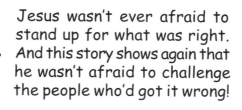

Jesus wasn't ever afraid to stand up for what was right. And this story shows again that he wasn't afraid to challenge the people who'd got it wrong!

LUKE 13:10-17

One Sabbath day, when Jesus was teaching in the synagogue, he saw a woman who had been crippled by an evil spirit. She had been bent double for eighteen years and could not stand up straight. Jesus called the woman over and said, "Woman, you are healed of your sickness." He touched her, and from that moment she could stand up straight. How she praised and thanked God.

The leader in charge of the synagogue was most displeased that Jesus had healed her on the Sabbath day. "There are six days of the week for working," he said. "You should come on those days to be healed, not on the Sabbath." But Jesus said, "You hypocrite! You untie your ox or donkey and lead it out to water on the Sabbath without giving it a thought!" This woman has been held in bondage by Satan for many years. Wasn't it necessary for me to free her?" This shamed Jesus' enemies. And all the people rejoiced at the wonderful things he did.

Answer the following questions and fill in the gaps. Then put the starred letters together to find out the number of years that the woman had been crippled. 1. Jesus was doing this when the woman came. 2. How many working days? 3. Jesus was in this place of worship. 4. The woman did this to God when she was healed. 5. The day when Jesus healed the woman. 6. They were shamed. 7. The people did this when they saw what happened. 8. An animal in the story.

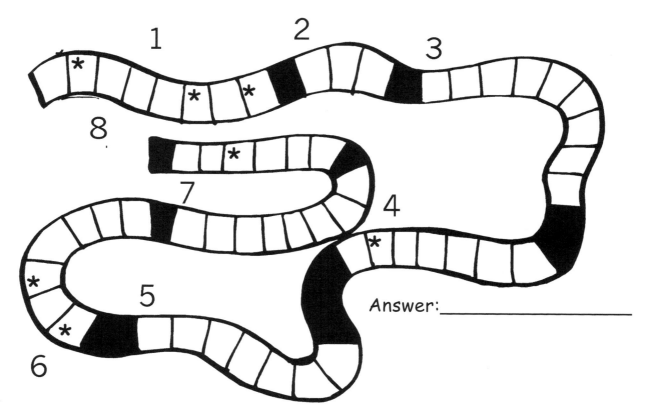

Answer:_____

THE STORY OF THE GREAT FEAST

LUKE 14:15-24

Everywhere that Jesus went he made people think about why they did things. Like, if they were going to give a meal, he said not to invite friends, family or rich neighbours who could invite them back. Instead, he said to invite the poor, the crippled, the lame and the blind. Those people couldn't repay the kindness, but God would reward. And Jesus told a story. A man prepared a wonderful feast and he sent out lots of invitations. When the feast was ready, he sent out his servant to tell the guests that it was time to come. But they all began making excuses. Fill the gaps with a,e,i,o or u.

1

I'v - j - st g - t m - rr - - d s - - c - n't c - m -.

I'v - b - - ght - f - - ld - nd - w - nt t - - nsp - ct - t.

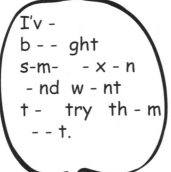

I'v - b - - ght s-m- - x - n - nd w - nt t - try th - m - - t.

2

3

Well, as you can guess, when the servant got back and told his master what they'd said, he was very angry. Fill in the a,e,i,o and u vowels to see what he said.

G - q - - ckly - nt - th - str - - ts - nd - ll - ys - f th - c - ty - nd - nv - t - th - p - - r, th - cr - ppl - d, th - l - m - - nd th - bl - nd.

The servant did this, and there was still room for more. So the master said: "Go out into the lanes and behind the hedges. Encourage anyone you find to come so that the house will be full. Not one of those I invited first will get the smallest taste of what I prepared for them."

THE LOST SON

We're onto chapter 15 now - and it's about a family who were having problems.

A man had two sons. One day the younger son said, "Father, I want my share of your estate now and not when you die." So his father agreed. A few days later, the younger son packed his belongings, went to a distant land and wasted all his money on wild living.

When his money ran out a famine swept over the land and he began to starve. He had to work as a pig feeder and was so hungry that even the pigs food looked tasty. At last he came to his senses and he said, "Even the hired men at home have enough food to eat, and here am I, dying of hunger. I'll go home to my father and say, 'Father, I've sinned against heaven and you. I'm not worthy to be called your son, but please take me on as your hired hand'." So he went home, and while he was still some way away, his father saw him coming.

Filled with love he ran to greet his son and hugged him and kissed him. Turning to his servants he said, "Quick! Bring the best robe and put it on him. Get a ring for his finger and sandals for his feet. We will kill the calf we've been fattening. Let's celebrate. For my son was dead and has now come back to life. He was lost but now he's found. And so a party began.

When the older son came back from working in the fields, he heard music and dancing. And when he heard what had happened he was so angry he wouldn't go in. "All these years I've worked hard for you," he said to his father. "I did everything you asked. Yet you never gave even a young goat for a feast with my friends. Now my brother comes back after spending all his money foolishly. And you celebrate by killing our best calf." His father said to him. "Dear son. Everything I have is yours. We had to celebrate. For your brother was dead and has come back to life. He was lost, but now he is found."

Can you help the lost son find his father?

THE SHREWD MANAGER

Here's another story Jesus told. Work out the order of the papers by referring to your bibles. Number each piece as you go.

The man replied "800 gallons of olive oil."
"Then tear up that bill and write another for 400 gallons," he said.

A rich man hired a manager to look after his affairs. But soon a rumour went round that the manager was thoroughly dishonest.

The rich man couldn't help admiring his manager for being so smart. And it's true that the world's citizens are more streetwise than the godly. Jesus said, "use your worldly things to benefit others and make friends. And your generosity will store up a reward for you in heaven."

So the manager was called in to his employer, who said, "What's this I hear about your stealing from me? I will dismiss you, so you'd better get your work in order."

The manager thought to himself, "Now what shall I do? I don't have strength to dig ditches. I'm too proud to beg. I know. I'll fix it so that I have plenty of friends to look after me when I leave."

So the manager invited everyone who owed money to his employer to come and discuss the situation. "How much do you owe?" he asked the first.

"And how much do you owe?" he asked the next. "1000 bushels of wheat," the man replied. "Here," said the manager, "Take your bill and replace it with one for 800 bushels."

Work out what words these pictures are and fit them into the gaps in the sentences on the following page.

Jesus then gave some wise sayings. Can you fill in the gaps?

Unless you are - - - - - - - - in small things, you won't be faithful in large ones.

If you cheat even a little you won't be - - - - - - with greater responsibilities. If you are not trustworthy about wordly wealth, who will trust you with the riches of - - - - - -. If you aren't faithful with other people's money, why should you be - - - - - - - with your own.

THE RICH MAN AND LAZARUS

Hey Harry - look at this. Here's a story about a rich man and a beggar.

There was a rich man who lived in luxury. At his door lay a diseased beggar called Lazarus. He would lie by the rich man's house, longing for scraps of food from the rich man's table. As he lay there, the dogs would come and lick his open sores.

Finally, the beggar died, and was carried by the angels to be with Abraham in heaven. The rich man died too, and his soul was taken to Hades, the place of the dead. There, in torment, he looked into the distance and saw Lazarus with Abraham. "Father Abraham," cried the rich man. "Have pity on me. Send Lazarus to dip the tip of his finger in water and cool my tongue. I am in agony in these flames." Abraham replied, "Son, remember that while you were alive you had everything you wanted and Lazarus had nothing. Now he is being comforted while you suffer. And besides, there is a deep pit separating us. No one can cross over to you from here and no-one from there can cross over to us."

Then the rich man said, "Send Lazarus to my father's home. I have five brothers and I want to warn them about this terrible place so that they don't come here when they die." But Abraham said, "Moses and the prophets have warned them. Your brothers can read their writings and find out for themselves." The rich man said, "But Father Abraham, if someone from the dead is sent to them they will turn from their sins." And Abraham replied, "If they won't listen to Moses and the prophets, they won't listen even if someone comes back from the dead."

Can you answer the following questions? Take the first letter of each answer and write it in the apple with the same number. The answer will tell you what Lazarus was enjoying in heaven with Abraham.

Questions

1. They were causing the rich man great pain.
2. The Rich man when alive lived in luxury _ _ _ _ _ _ _ _.
3. They carried Lazarus away.
4. The rich man wanted his brothers to turn away from them.
5. The rich man wanted to cool it.

THE STORY OF THE PERSISTENT WIDOW

Luke 18: 1-8

Jess and I have found out that prayer was very important to Jesus.

Yes, that's right - and he told this story to encourage the disciples to pray and never give up.

There was a judge in a certain town. He didn't fear God and he didn't respect people. In the same town there was also a widow, and she kept coming to him and asking for justice against someone who had harmed her. The judge ignored the woman for a while, until at last, she wore him out. "I don't fear God or man," said the judge, "but this woman is driving me crazy. I'm going to make sure that she gets her rights or she will wear me out with her requests." Jesus said, "Learn a lesson from this judge. Even though he was evil, he made sure that justice was done. Now, don't you think that God will judge us in favour of his own chosen people who cry out to him for help day and night. He will judge in their favour quickly. But when I, the Son of Man return, how many will I find who have such faith?"

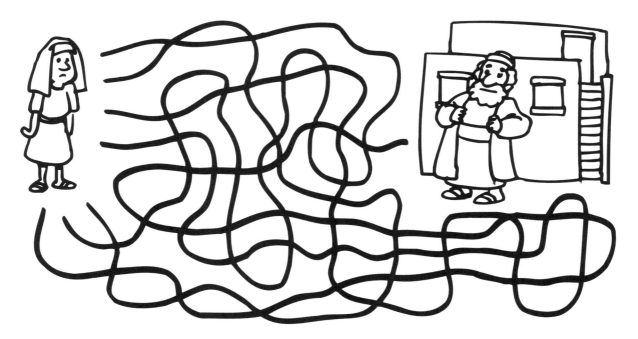

Follow the wiggly lines. Which one leads to the judge's house?

JESUS PREDICTS HIS DEATH

Jesus often warned the disciples that something terrible was going to happen to him.

LUKE 18: 31-34

HOLY BIBLE

But even though he told them, they didn't understand because the meaning of the words had been hidden from them. This is what he said.

"As you know, we are going to Jerusalem and everything the prophets said about the Son of Man will come true. He will be handed over to the Romans who will mock him, insult him and spit on him. They will whip and kill him, but 3 days later he will rise to life."

Answer the following questions. Then put the first letters of each answer together to discover Jesus' final destination.

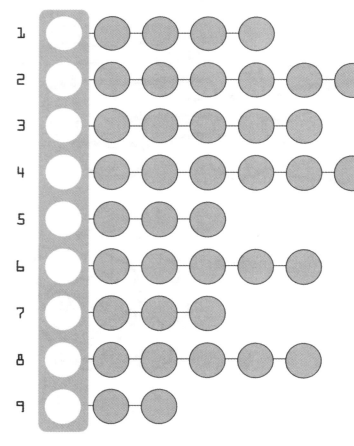

1. Who was speaking?
2. How much would come true?
3. Jesus would be their prisoner.
4. The disciples didn't - - - - - - - - - - the meaning.
5. People would do this to Jesus.
6. A disciple of Jesus.
7. Jesus would rise to - - - -.
8. How many disciples, minus one.
9. Jesus was the Son of - - -.

Answer_____

42

THE STORY OF THE TEN SERVANTS

Jesus and his followers were almost at Jerusalem. The people thought that the kingdom of God was just about to appear, so Jesus told a story.

A King was once called to a country far away. He gave each of his ten servants a gold coin, and expected them to earn extra with the money while he was away. However the king's subjects hated him and they sent messengers after him to say that they didn't want him to be king. The king returned, and he called each of his servants to find out how much they earned.

Follow the wiggly lines and find out what the king said to the servants.

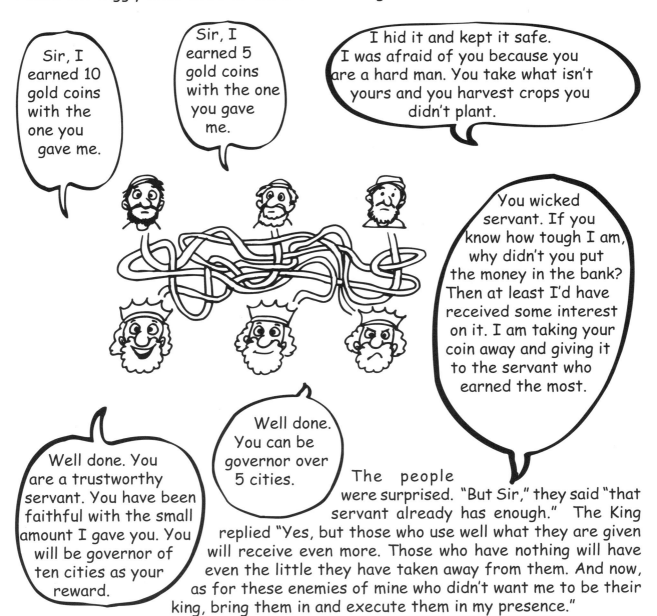

Sir, I earned 10 gold coins with the one you gave me.

Sir, I earned 5 gold coins with the one you gave me.

I hid it and kept it safe. I was afraid of you because you are a hard man. You take what isn't yours and you harvest crops you didn't plant.

You wicked servant. If you know how tough I am, why didn't you put the money in the bank? Then at least I'd have received some interest on it. I am taking your coin away and giving it to the servant who earned the most.

Well done. You are a trustworthy servant. You have been faithful with the small amount I gave you. You will be governor of ten cities as your reward.

Well done. You can be governor over 5 cities.

The people were surprised. "But Sir," they said "that servant already has enough." The King replied "Yes, but those who use well what they are given will receive even more. Those who have nothing will have even the little they have taken away from them. And now, as for these enemies of mine who didn't want me to be their king, bring them in and execute them in my presence."

WORD SEARCH

Can you find the following words: king, servant, gold, coins, bank, crops, five, ten, cities, reward.

S	A	P	R	S	O	N	I	N	S
O	M	S	N	E	S	P	O	R	C
I	L	E	W	A	W	B	X	A	I
D	U	R	I	T	O	A	A	K	R
N	T	V	G	O	L	D	R	N	E
V	C	A	E	P	A	I	S	D	K
F	O	N	F	I	V	E	T	U	I
O	I	T	R	B	O	V	O	E	L
A	N	H	C	I	T	I	E	S	N
W	S	E	G	N	I	K	P	S	G

44

JESUS' TRIUMPHAL ENTRY

Luke 19: 28-40

After telling this story, Jesus went on to Jerusalem, walking ahead of his disciples. When they were getting close to the two towns called Bethphage and Bethany, he sent two disciples ahead.

"Go ahead into that village over there," he said. "As you enter it you'll see a colt tied up which has never been ridden. Untie it and bring it here. If anyone asks what you are doing, say that the Lord needs it." So the disciples went on and found the colt. As they were untying it the owners asked what they were doing. "The Lord needs it," they replied. And they brought the colt to Jesus, throwing their garments over it for Jesus to ride on. As Jesus rode along, the crowds spread their coats on the road ahead of him. Jesus' followers shouted and sang, praising God for all the miracles they had seen. "God bless the king who comes in the name of the Lord. Peace in heaven and glory to God." Some of the Pharisees in the crowd spoke to Jesus, saying, "Teacher, tell your disciples to be quiet." But Jesus said, "I tell you, if they keep quiet, the stones along the road will start shouting.

Using the colour code key colour in the picture of the donkey below.

1 - light blue
2 - dark blue
3 - light green
4 - dark green
5 - orange
6 - yellow
7 - grey
8 - brown

JESUS CLEARS THE TEMPLE

One day Jesus went into the temple in Jerusalem. He drove the merchants out from their stalls. Jesus had good reason to do this. He said, "The scriptures say, "My house will be a house of prayer," but you have made it a den of robbers." Jesus was angry because people were acting dishonestly. He said that they'd turned the temple into a "den of thieves." After this the leading priests began planning how to kill him.

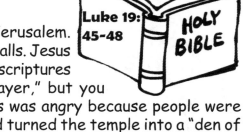

Luke 19: 45-48

HOLY BIBLE

THE STORY OF THE EVIL FARMERS

Here's another story from Jesus. Can you find a mouse, bird, rabbit and, worm in the pictures?
A man planted a vineyard and let it out to tenants. Then

Luke 20: 9-19

HOLY BIBLE

he moved to another country to live for several years. When it was harvest time he sent a servant to collect his share of the crop. But the farmers beat him up and sent him back empty. The owner sent another and another and each time they were beaten up and thrown out. "What shall I do?" thought the owner. "I know, I will send my own dear son. They will respect him." When the farmers saw his son, they said. "Here comes his son. Let's kill him and get the estate for ourselves." So they dragged him out of the vineyard and murdered him. Jesus said, "What will the owner do? He will kill those men and hand the vineyard over to others." When the people heard this, they said, "God forbid that this could happen." But the leading priests heard the story and wanted to arrest Jesus. They knew that they were like the farmers in the story. But they were afraid that there would be a riot if they arrested him. So they watched and waited for an opportunity.

JESUS ABOUT TO BE BETRAYED

We're on chapter 22 now and it's the Passover festival. The leading priests are still plotting to murder Jesus. We've found out that Satan has entered one of the disciples. He went to the leading priests and captains of the temple guard and discussed the best way to betray Jesus to them.

Of course, they were really pleased - they even promised him a reward. So he began to look for an opportunity to betray Jesus at a time when the crowds weren't around.
Who was he?
Use the code to find out.

Answer: _____

JESUS PREPARES TO EAT THE PASSOVER MEAL

We've found out that the Passover or Festival of Unleavened Bread was quite an important time. It was on this particular day that lambs for the Passover meal were to be killed. And on this day, Jesus sent Peter and John to go ahead and get the Passover meal ready. Peter and John said, "Where do you want us to get it ready?" Match up the paper scraps to find out Jesus' instructions.

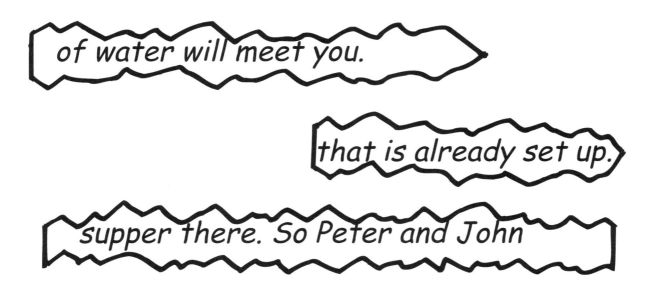

Go into the city. A man carrying a jar

Follow him
and go into the house that he enters.
Say to the

"The teacher asks,
where is the room where I can eat the

disciples?" He
will take you upstairs to a large room

You go ahead and prepare our

went off and found everything just as
Jesus had told them.

owner of the house,

Passover meal with my

THE LAST SUPPER

At the proper time, Jesus sat down at the table with the twelve disciples. He said, "I have wanted so much to eat this Passover meal with you before my suffering begins. For I can tell you now that I won't eat it again until it is given its full meaning in the kingdom of God."

Then Jesus took a cup and gave thanks to God. He said, "Take this and share it among yourselves. I will not drink wine again until the kingdom of God has come." Jesus took some bread. He gave thanks to God, broke it into pieces and gave it to his disciples. "This is my body, given for you," he said. "Do this in memory of me." After supper, Jesus took another cup of wine and said, "This wine is the token of God's new covenant to save you. It is sealed with the blood I will pour out for you. But look! The one who will betray me is sitting here at the table among us. I will die as it is God's plan. But how terrible for the one who betrays me." Then they began to ask each other which of them would ever do such a thing.

Click has downloaded another puzzle. Answer the following questions and the vertical column will reveal a name Jesus gave himself.

1. The meal was a celebration of this festival.
2. Kingdom of _ _ _.
3. The disciples drank it with Jesus.
4. A disciple.
5. For Jesus, it was about to begin.
6. Do this in _ _ _ _ _ _ of me.
7. One of the disciples would do this to Jesus.
8. Something new which was God's promise to save them.

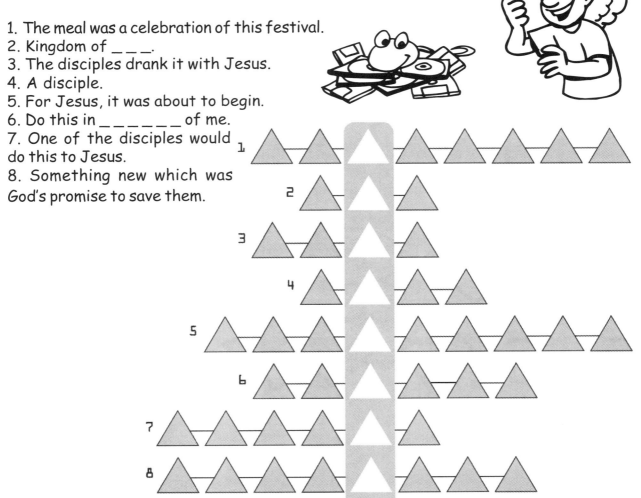

JESUS PREDICTS PETER'S DENIAL

Jesus knew that Simon-Peter was going to deny him, but he wanted to encourage him not to give up. Fill in the gaps by matching the shapes.

Luke 22:31-38

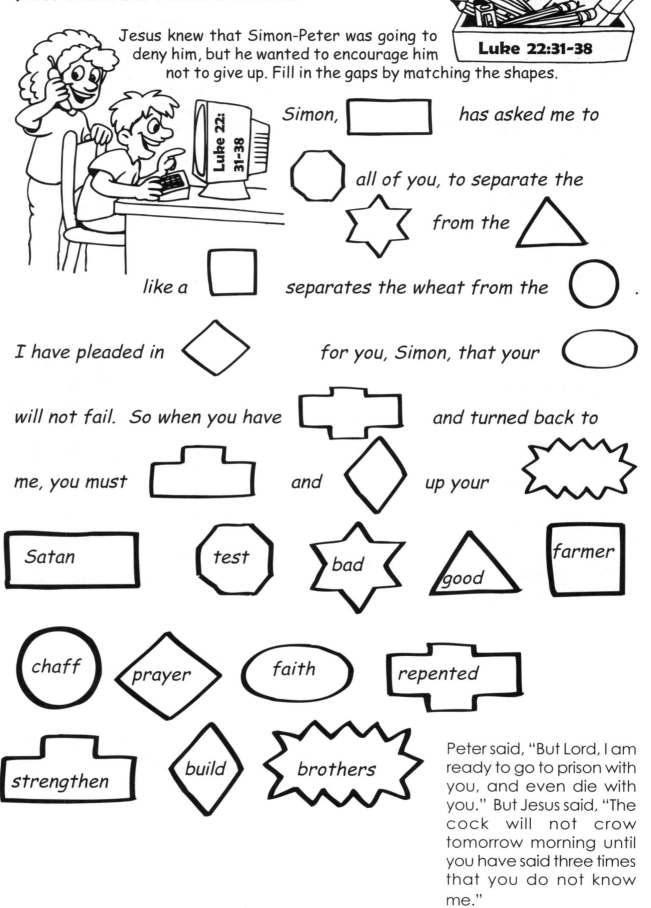

Luke 22: 31-38

Simon, [rectangle] has asked me to [octagon] all of you, to separate the [star] from the [triangle] like a [square] separates the wheat from the [circle].

I have pleaded in [diamond] for you, Simon, that your [oval] will not fail. So when you have [cross shape] and turned back to me, you must [T-shape] and [diamond] up your [starburst].

Satan — test — bad — good — farmer

chaff — prayer — faith — repented

strengthen — build — brothers

Peter said, "But Lord, I am ready to go to prison with you, and even die with you." But Jesus said, "The cock will not crow tomorrow morning until you have said three times that you do not know me."

50

JESUS PRAYS ON THE MOUNT OF OLIVES

So Jesus and the disciples left the upstairs room and went to the Mount of Olives. And Jesus said to them, "Pray that you won't be overcome by temptation." Then Jesus walked about a stone's throw away and knelt and prayed. Click has downloaded Jesus' words for us but some words are missing. Fill in the gaps by taking the initial letters of the objects, working out the words and then placing them in the right gap in the sentence.

"__ __ __ __ __ __, IF YOU ARE __ __ __ __ __ __ __, PLEASE TAKE THIS

__ __ __ OF __ __ __ __ __ __ __ __ __ AWAY FROM ME, YET I WANT YOUR

__ __ __ __, NOT MINE."

An angel from heaven came and strengthened him. Jesus prayed even more fervently and his sweat fell to the ground like great drops of blood. At last he got up and went back to the disciples and found them asleep, worn out from their grief. "Why are you sleeping?" he said, "Get up and pray otherwise temptation will overpower you."

JESUS IS BETRAYED AND ARRESTED

Things did not look good. Over to Click.....

While Jesus was still speaking, a crowd led by Judas arrived. Judas came up to Jesus to kiss him. And Jesus said, "Judas, is it with a kiss that you betray the Son of Man?" The other disciples saw what was about to happen and said, "Lord, shall we fight? We brought swords with us." And one of them cut off the right ear of the High Priest's servant. Jesus said, "Enough!" He touched the man's ear and healed him. Then Jesus spoke to the chief priests and officers of the temple guard who had come to get him. "Did you have to come with swords and clubs to arrest me, as if I am some dangerous criminal? I was with you every day in the temple, but you didn't arrest me then. But this is your moment when the power of darkness rules."

PETER DENIES JESUS

So Jesus was arrested and taken to the High Priest's house. Peter followed from a distance. There was a fire which had been lit in the courtyard and Peter joined the people sitting round it. A servant girl saw Peter. Look at what she said and then use the code to work out what Peter said in reply.

Luke 22: 54-62

23, 15, 13, 1, 14   9   4, 15, 14, 20   5, 22, 5, 14
11, 14, 15, 23   8, 9, 13

a = 1
b = 2
c = 3   etc.

After a while, a man saw Peter. Look at what he said and work out what Peter replied.

13, 1, 14   9   1, 13
14, 15, 20

This man was with Jesus too.

Then, around an hour later, another man spoke to Peter. Here is what he said and again - work out what Peter replied.

13, 1, 14   9   4, 15, 14, 20
11, 14, 15, 23   23, 8, 1, 20
25, 15, 21   1, 18, 5
20, 1, 12, 11, 9, 14, 7
1, 2, 15, 21, 20!

You are one of them too.

There's no doubt that this man was with Jesus because he is a Galilean!

As soon as he's said it a cock crowed, and Jesus turned round and looked straight at him. He remembered that Jesus had said he would betray him 3 times before the cock crowed and left the courtyard weeping bitterly.

JESUS BEFORE THE COUNCIL

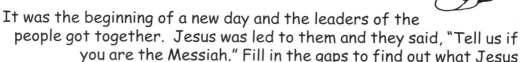

It was the beginning of a new day and the leaders of the people got together. Jesus was led to them and they said, "Tell us if you are the Messiah." Fill in the gaps to find out what Jesus said.

Luke 22: 66-71

a = #   e = *   & = i   ^ = o   ~ = u

&f & t*ll y^~, y^~ w^n't b*l&*v*

m*. #nd &f & #sk y^~ #   q~*st&^n y^~ w^nt

#nsw*r m*. B~t th* t&m* &s c^m&ng wh*n &, th*

S^n ^f M#n w&ll b* s&tt&ng #t G^d's r&ght h#nd &n th* pl#c*

^f p^w*r.

They didn't like this at all. "So you claim that you are the Son of God?" they said. And Jesus said, "You are right in saying that I am." "Well, we don't need witnesses - we've heard him say it ourselves," they said. So Jesus was taken to Pilate, the Roman governor.

JESUS IS BROUGHT BEFORE PILATE

Luke 23: 1-7

This man's been telling the people not to pay taxes to the Roman government. He says that he's a king.

Are you the King of the Jews?

Of course, Jesus didn't deny it.

I find nothing wrong with this man.

Look at what the council said against Jesus...

He causes riots everywhere he goes, from Galilee to Jerusalem.

And when Pilate learned that Jesus was a Galilean he sent him to Herod, the ruler over that region. It seems that Herod was in Jerusalem too.

JESUS BEFORE HEROD

It seems that Herod was really pleased that Jesus had been sent to him. He'd heard a lot about him and was hoping to see him perform a miracle. Herod asked Jesus loads of questions but he wouldn't answer. And all this time, the leading priests and teachers of religious law shouted accusations against Jesus.

Follow the wiggly lines to find out what happened next.

Herod   his   mocked   ridiculed   They   a royal   on   and   him   to

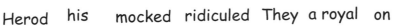

put   Jesus.   robe   and   him   back   Pilate.   soldiers   sent   and

JESUS IS SENTENCED TO DEATH

So Pilate said to the leading priests and people, "You've accused this man of leading a revolt. I have examined him and find him innocent. Herod thinks the same and has sent him back." Pilate said that he would have Jesus whipped and set free. But there was a huge roar from the crowds. Work out what they said.

Luke 23:13-25

Pilate said, "Why? What crime has he committed? I have no reason to sentence him to death. I'll flog him and let him go." But the crowd shouted louder and louder for Jesus' to be killed. Then Pilate sentenced Jesus to death and he set Barabbas free.

Barabbas had been in prison for murder.

THE CRUCIFIXION

Follow the footprints that link each part of the story. Colour in the right ones and piece together what happened.

Jesus was led away, and a man called Simon of Cyrene, who had come in from the country, was forced to carry Jesus' cross and walk behind him.

Two criminals were led out to be executed with Jesus. They were taken to a place called "The Skull" and all three were crucified there, with Jesus in the centre.

Luke 23: 26-43

Jesus said, "Father, forgive these people because they don't know what they're doing." And the soldiers gambled for his clothes by throwing dice.

The crowd watched while the leaders laughed and scoffed. "He saved others," they said, "If he is God's chosen Messiah, let him save himself."

One of the criminals hanging beside Jesus shouted insults at him. "So you are the Messiah are you? Well prove it by saving yourself, and us!"

Above Jesus was written, "This is the King of the Jews."

The soldiers also mocked him, by offering him a drink with sour wine. "If you are the king of the Jews save yourself," they said.

But the other one said, "Don't you fear God? We deserve to die for what we did, but this man hasn't done anything wrong."

Then he said to Jesus, "Remember me when you come into your kingdom."

And Jesus said, "I promise that today you will be in paradise with me."

The End

55

THE DEATH OF JESUS

Luke 23: 44-49

At noon, darkness fell across the whole land until 3 o'clock. Then, suddenly, the curtain in the temple was torn apart. Jesus shouted, "Father, In your hands I place my spirit!" With those words, he died. When the captain of the Roman soldiers saw what had happened, he praised God and said...

Use the clocks to work out what he said.

6pm,8pm,5pm,4am,11am,11pm

7pm,7am,8am,6pm

12pm,12am,1pm 10pm,12am,6pm

5pm, 8am, 6am, 7am, 7pm, 4am,
2pm, 8pm, 6pm.

Answer:_____

THE BURIAL OF JESUS

When the people who had come to see the crucifixion saw what had happened, they went home with deep sadness. But Jesus' friends, including the women who had followed him from Galilee, stood at a distance watching. Click has found an account of what happened after Jesus had died. Let's find out what happened!

There was once an honourable man named Joseph from Arimathea. He was a member of the Jewish high council, but did not agree with the decisions or actions of the other leaders. Joseph went to Pilate and asked for Jesus' body. He took it down from the cross, wrapped it in a linen sheet and laid it in a new tomb carved out of rock. It was Friday, and the Sabbath was about to begin. As Jesus' body was taken away, the

women who had come with Jesus from Galilee followed. Then they went home and prepared spices and perfumes for his body. On the Sabbath day they rested as the law commanded.

Luke 23: 50-55

THE RESURRECTION

Early on the Sunday morning the women set out for the tomb carrying the spices. What a shock they had when they got there! Here's what we've found out.

They found that the stone covering the entrance had been rolled away. They went in, and were puzzled to find that Jesus' body was not there. Suddenly, two men in bright, shining clothes stood before them. The women were terrified and bowed down to the ground. The men asked, "Why are you looking among the dead for someone who is alive? Don't you remember what he said to you when he was in Galilee? The Son of Man would be handed over to sinful men and be crucified. Three days later he would rise to life." Then the women remembered that he had said this. They rushed back to tell the eleven disciples and everyone else what had happened. They were Mary Magdalene, Joanna and Mary the mother of James. The disciples thought that the story was nonsense and did not believe the women. However, Peter ran to the tomb for a look. He found the linen wrappings, then went back home, wondering what had happened.

Match the spice bottles and spell a message that the angels gave the women at the tomb. Then fill in the gap in the story.

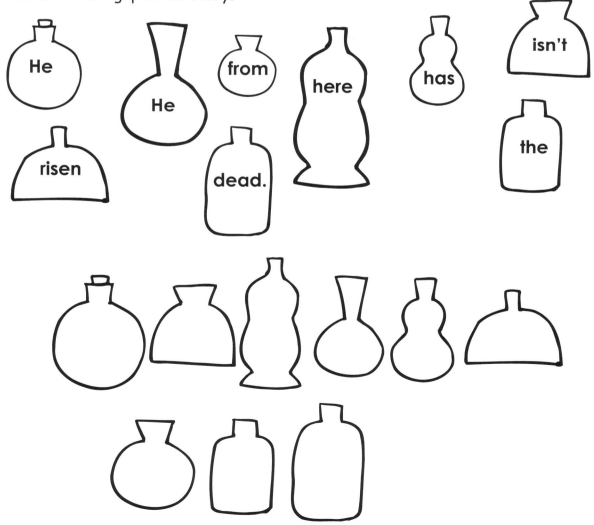

THE WALK TO EMMAUS

That same day, two of Jesus' followers had a big surprise while they journeyed to Emmaus, a short way from Jerusalem. They were talking about all the things that had happened, when Jesus came and started walking with them. But - they didn't recognise him! Here's a print-out of what happened.

Luke 24: 13-35

Jesus asked the two men what they were talking about, and they stopped, their faces full of sadness. "You must be the only person in Jerusalem who hasn't heard about all the things that have happened over the last few days," said Cleopas, one of the men.

"What things?" asked Jesus.

"The things that happened to Jesus of Nazareth," they answered, and they explained what had happened. They told Jesus about the women who had found the tomb empty, and about the angels' message.

Then Jesus said, "How foolish you are, and how slow to believe what the prophets said. Wasn't it necessary for the Messiah to suffer these things before entering his time of glory?" Then Jesus explained passages from the writings of Moses and the prophets, explaining what the scriptures had said about him.

By this time they were nearing Emmaus. They begged Jesus to stay the night with them as it was getting late. So he sat down to eat with them. He took some bread, asked God's blessing on it, broke it and gave it to them. Then their eyes were opened and they recognised him. And at that moment he disappeared.

They said to each other, "Weren't our hearts strangely warm as he talked with us on the road?" And they got up and returned to Jerusalem, where they found the eleven disciples. When they arrived, they were told, "The Lord has really risen! He has appeared to Peter."

JESUS APPEARS TO THE DISCIPLES AND THE ASCENSION

As the two men were speaking, Jesus came and stood among them. Here is what happened next...

"Peace be with you," he said. The whole group were terrified, thinking that they were seeing a ghost. But Jesus said, "Why are you frightened? Why do you doubt who I am?

Luke 24:36-53

Look at my hands and feet and you can see it's really me. Touch me and you'll know, because ghosts don't have bodies like I do!" And as he spoke, Jesus held out his hands and showed them his feet. Still they doubted, yet they were filled with joy and wonder. Then Jesus said, "Do you have anything to eat?" They gave him cooked fish and he ate it as they watched. Jesus said, "When I was with you before, I told you that everything written about me by Moses and the prophets had come true." Then he went on to help them understand the scriptures. Jesus said, "It was written long ago that the Messiah must suffer and die and rise again on the third day. You are my witnesses, and with my authority, take this message of repentance to all the nations, starting in Jerusalem. There is forgiveness of sins for all who turn to me. Now I will send my Holy Spirit, just as my Father promised. But stay here until the Holy Spirit comes and fills you with power from heaven."

Jesus made an amazing promise that there would be forgiveness for sins if people turn to him. You can see it written below, but can you fill in the right answers?

1. Jesus ate it in front of the disciples.
2. They would receive this from (14) just as the Father had promised.
3. The subject of the message to the nations.
4. The disciples thought at first that they were seeing one.
5. The disciples felt this when they first saw Jesus.
6. _ _ _ _ us each day our daily bread. Luke 11:3
7. Before Jesus was born, he talked about him in the scriptures.
8. The gospel was to go out to them.
9. They were to begin in this city.
10. Jesus helped the disciples to understand them.
11. The Messiah must _ _ _ _ _ _ before he died.
12. Ghosts don't have them like Jesus did.
13. Jesus showed them to his disciples.
14. Father, Son and Holy _ _ _ _ _ _.
15. The disciples were to be this with Jesus' authority.
16. The disciples were filled with this when they'd touched Jesus.
17. A command Jesus gave them before the Holy Spirit came.

Then Jesus led them to Bethany where he raised his hands and blessed them. While he was blessing them he was taken up to heaven. They worshipped him, then went back to Jerusalem, filled with great joy. They spent all their time in the temple, giving thanks to God. And that's how Luke's gospel ends. We hope you've enjoyed the journey with us. And if you've enjoyed this, why not explore another gospel with us. Bye!

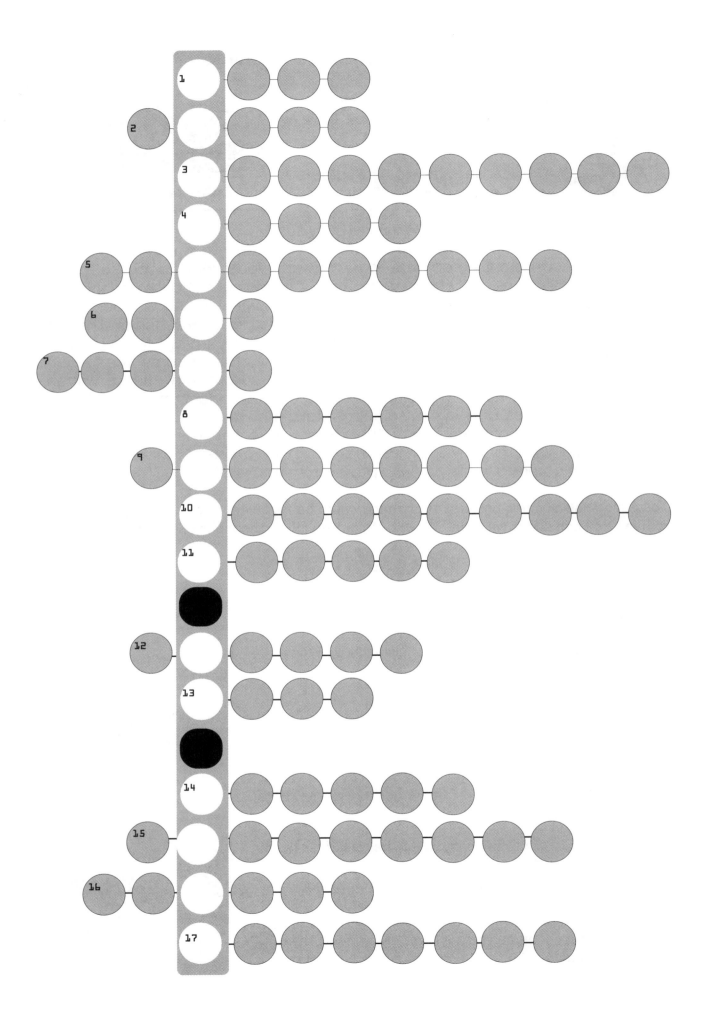

Answers

News of a birth - Page 3 - You will have great joy and gladness many will rejoice with you at his birth. He will be great in the eyes of the Lord he will be filled with the Holy Spirit even before his birth. He will persuade many Israelites to turn to the Lord their God. He will be a man with the spirit of power of Elijah, the prophet of old. He will prepare the people for the coming of the Lord.

Mary and Gabriel - Page 4 - You will become pregnant and have a son and you are to name him Jesus. I am the Lord's servant, and I am willing to accept whatever he wants. May everything you have said come true.

Shepherds and Angels - Page 6 - Spot the Difference - Card 1 - Shepherds in white clothes, 1 white sheep 1 black sheep; Card 2 Shepherd with black belt and band, shephered with black hat; angel; two black sheep; Card three - shepherd with black head scarf; three angels; a star, shepherd with black robe; one black eared white sheep.

Jesus is presented at the temple - Page 7 - Lord, now I can depart in peace! For my eyes have seen your salvation which you have prepared in the sight of all people, a light to reveal God to the nations, and he is the glory of your people Israel. *Messiah;* (Immanuel) This child is destined to cause the falling and rising of many in Israel, and to be a sign that will be spoken against, so that the thoughts of many hearts will be revealed. And a sword will pierce your own soul too. .

Jesus speaks with the teachers - Page 8 - (1) deep (2) frantic (3) festival (4) answers (5) house (6) relatives (7) temple (8) Nazareth. Ans: Passover

John the Baptist prepares the way - Page 9 - You are my beloved son and I am fully pleased with you.

Jesus rejected at Nazareth - Page 10 - Good News; Downtrodden; Crossword Across: (1) scroll (5) preach (7) Isaiah (9) favour (12) news (13) crowd (14) he (15) today (19) freed (20) Elisha Down: (2) read (3) rain (4) Christ (6) returned (8) amazed (10) good (11) away (13) cliff (14) home (16) acid (17) heal (18) see

Jesus casts out a demon - Page 12 - What authority and power this man's words possess! Even evil spirits obey him and flee at his command.

The first disciples - Page 13 - Don't be afraid. From now on you'll be fishing for people.

Jesus calls Levi - Page 14 - Healthy people don't need a doctor, sick people do. I have come to call sinners to turn from their sins, not to spend my time with those who think they are already good enough.

Jesus chooses twelve - Page 15 - Matthew; Bartholomew; Philip; John; James; Simon Peter; Andrew; Judas Iscariot; Simon; Judas; Thomas.

Crowds follow Jesus - Page 16 - Sidon; Tyre; Jerusalem.

The Faith of the Roman Officer - **Page 17** - I have not found such great faith even in Israel.

Jesus raises a widow's son - Page 18 - Find the camel and the well; the dog and the rabbit; the cat and the mouse; the donkey and the tree.

Jesus anointed by a sinful woman - Page 19 and 20 - Your sins are forgiven; Crossword Across: (1) water (3) Kneeling (5) meal (6) wash (8) home (9) sent (11) saved (13) sat (15) debt (16) olive (18) eat (20) loan (24) below (25) jar (26) faith (27) if (28) entered (32) hair (33) key (34) save

Jesus anointed ... Crossword Down: (1) woman (2) tears (3) kiss (4) greeting (6) weeping (7) head (10) table (12) anoint (14) immoral (17) go ahead (19) ate (21) love (22) offer (23) Simon (24) both (29) rare (30) dust (31) say (32) he

Women who followed Jesus - Page 21 - To announce the good news concerning the kingdom of God. Joanna, Mary Magdalene, Susanna

Jesus heals in reponse to faith - Page 22 and 23 - (1) John (2) peace (3) faith (4) afraid (5) touched (6) asleep Answer: Jairus

Jesus sends out the twelve - Page 24 - walking stick, travellers bag, food, money coat, home, message, dust, feet. Don't take a walking stick or a traveller's bag, nor food, nor money. Not even an extra coat. When you enter the village be a guest in only one home. If the people of the village won't receive your message when you enter it, shake off its dust from your feet as you leave. It's a sign that you have abandoned that village to its fate.

Sayings of Jesus - Page 25 - If any of you wants to be my follower, you must put aside selfish ambition, shoulder your cross daily and follow me. Lifebelt puzzle - If you try to keep your life for yourself you will lose it. But if you give up your life for me you will find true life.

The Transfiguration - Pages 26 & 27 - This is my son, my chosen one. Listen to him. Word search

The cost of following Jesus - Page 27 - Foxes have dens to live in and birds have nests, but I, the Son of Man have no home of my own; Let those who are spiritually dead care for their own dead; Anyone who puts a hand to the plough and then looks back is not fit for the kingdom of God.

The Good Samaritan - Pages 29-31 - You must love the Lord your God, with all your heart, all your soul, all your strength and all your mind and love your neighbour as yourself. Spot the Differences. 1st set of pictures - rabbit is in then out; patch on one eye then on the other; star above then below; injured man squints and then doesn't squint. 2nd set of pictures - White hat/black hat; White robe/black robe; butterfly/no butterfly; sun/no sun; Four snakes/three snakes. 3rd set of pictures - Scratch left ear/right ear; long beard/short beard; bag on ground/bag on shoulder 4th set of pictures - 3 bottles/1 bottle; black hat/white hat; thin beard/thick beard. 5th set of pictures - white hair/black hair; mouse/no mouse; white blanket/black blanket; white headscarf/black headscarf.

Jesus criticises the religious leaders - Page 32 & 33 - Crossword Across: (1) trap (3) murder (6) life (8) table (11) vine (12) all (14) Abel (15) tie (16) teacher (18) God (19) key (20) cup (23) experts (24) hide (28) dish (31) love (32) sat (33) altar (34) west (35) markets (36) stern. Down: (1) tithe (2) give (3) men (4) death (5) ruler (7) filthy (9) build (10) eat (13) lie (17) crush (18) greed (21) creation (22) cry (25) inside (26) core (27) seats (29) idea (30) hawk (31) laws.

The Rich Fool - Page 34 - You fool; die.

Jesus heals on the Sabbath- Page 35 - (1) teaching (2) six (3) synagogoue (4) thanked (5) sabbath (6) enemies (7) rejoiced (8) donkey Ans: Eighteen Years.

The story of the great feast - Page 36 - I've just got married so I can't come; I've bought some oxen and want to try them out; I've bought a field and want to inspect it./ Go quickly into the streets and alleys of the city and invite the poor the crippled, the lame and the blind.

The Shrewd Manager - Page 38 & 39- faithful, honest, heaven, trusted

The Rich Man and Lazarus - Page 39 and 40 - (1) flames (2) every day (3) angels (4) sins (5) tongue Answer: Feast.

Jesus predicts his death - Page 42 - (1) Jesus (2) everything (3) Romans (4) understand(5) spit (6) Andrew (7) life (8) eleven (9) man Ans: Jerusalem.

The story of the ten servants - Page 44- *Word search.*

Jesus about to be betrayed - Page 47 - Judas Iscariot.

Jesus prepares to eat the Passover Meal- Page 47 & 48 - Go into the city. A man carrying a jar of water will meet you. Follow him and go into the house that he enters. Say to the owner of the house "The Teacher asks, 'Where is the room where I can eat the Passover meal with my disciples?'" He will take you upstairs to a large room that is already set up. You go ahead and prepare our supper there. So Peter and John went and found everything just as Jesus had told them.

The Last Supper - Page 49 - (1) Passover (2) God (3) Wine 4) John (5) Suffering (6) memory (7) betray (8) covenant Ans: Son of Man

Jesus predicts Peter's Denial - Page 50 - Simon, Satan has asked me to test all of you, to separate the bad from the good like a farmer separates the wehat from the chaff. I have pleaded in prayer for you, Simon, that your faith will not fail. So when you have repented and turned back to me, you must strengthen and build up your brothers.

Jesus Prays on the Mount of Olives - Page 51 - Father, if you are willing, please take this cup of suffering away from me. Yet I want your will, not mine.

Peter denies Jesus - Page 52 - Woman, I don't even know him. Man, I am not. Man, I don't know what you are talking about.

Jesus before the council - Page 53 - If I tell you, you won't believe me. And if I ask you a question you won't answer me. But the time is coming when I, the Son of Man will be sitting at God's right hand in the place of power.

Jesus before Herod - Page 54 - Herod and his soldiers mocked and ridiculed Jesus. They put a royal robe on him and sent him back to Pilate.

Jesus is sentenced to death - Page 54 - Kill him and set Barabbas free.

The death of Jesus - Page 56 - Surely this man was righteous

The Resurrection - Page 57 - He isn't here! He has risen from the dead.

Jesus appears to the disciples and the Ascension - Pages 59 & 60 - (1) fish (2) power (3) repentance (4) ghost (5) frightened (6) give (7) Moses (8) Nations (9) Jerusalem (10) scriptures (11) suffer (12) bodies (13) feet (14) Spirit (15) witnesses (16) wonder (16) stay here. **Ans: Forgiveness.**

Word search Page 44

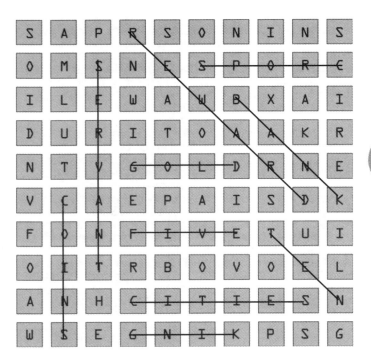

Word search Page 27

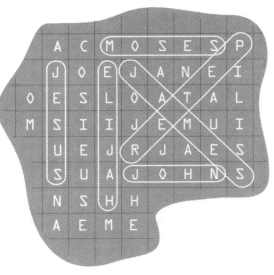

Certificate of Recognition

We've reached the end of the investigation Detectives! Well done everyone! Here is your certificate of Recognition. You deserve it!

As an official member of the Bible Detectives Squad you have been awarded this certificate to mark an excellent result!

Name:

_____

Investigation:

_____

Commenced on :

_____

Completed on:

_____

Signature:

_____

Meet the rest of the Gospel writers - Join the Bible Detectives Squad!
Matthew, Mark, Luke and John!

Good books with the real message of hope!

Christian Focus Publications publishes biblically-accurate books for adults and children. If you are looking for quality Bible teaching for children then we have a wide and excellent range of Bible story books - from board books to teenage fiction, we have it covered. You can also try our new Bible teaching Syllabus for 3-9 year olds and teaching materials for pre-school children.

These children's books are bright, fun and full of biblical truth, an ideal way to help children discover Jesus Christ for themselves. Our aim is to help children find out about God and get them enthusiastic about reading the Bible, now and later in their lives.

Find us at our web page:
www.christianfocus.com